The Let's Talk Library™

Let's Talk About Having a New Brother or Sister

Diana Star Helmer

The Rosen Publishing Group's
PowerKids Press™
New York

For Tom Owens, Don Middleton, Penny Weatherly, Miriam Landmark, Laura Dreasler, and Bruce and Mary Walker: Remember that somebody loves you.

Published in 1999 by The Rosen Publishing Group, Inc.
29 East 21st Street, New York, NY 10010

First Edition

Book Design: Erin McKenna

Photo Credits and Photo Illustrations: p. 4 © Maratea/International Stock; pp. 7, 15, 16, 20 Skjold Photographs; p. 8 by Seth Dinnerman; p. 11 by Carrie Ann Grippo; p. 12 by Ira Fox; p.19 by Maria Moreno.

Helmer, Diana Star, 1962–.
    Let's talk about having a new brother or sister/ by Diana Star Helmer.
        p.   cm.—(The let's talk library)
    Includes index.
    Summary: Helps the first-born child understand and deal with what happens when a new baby becomes part of the family.
    ISBN 0-8239-5191-X
    1. Infants—Juvenile literature. 2. Brothers and sisters—Juvenile literature.
    [1. Babies. 2. Brothers and sisters.] I. Title. II. Series.
    HQ774.H437 1998
    305.232—dc21   98–3525
                                                                                    CIP
                                                                                    AC

Manufactured in the United States of America

Table of Contents

A New Baby

Bruce and his mom were talking about the new baby.

"Will the baby cry ?" Bruce asked.

"All babies cry," Mom said. "Some babies cry a little more than others. Some cry less. We won't know until the baby is born. I think you'll like the baby more than you think you will."

"I already know that I'll like always having someone to play with!" Bruce said.

◀ A new baby can mean change for everybody in the family.

A New Brother or Sister

Having a new brother or sister is exciting. For about nine months your mom will be **pregnant** (PREG-nunt). You might be able to feel the new baby moving inside your mom's belly. But having a new brother or sister can be scary too. You might be afraid that you and your new brother or sister won't get along. Or you may worry that your parents will love your brother or sister more than you.

Your parents won't love the baby any more than they love you. You are their child, too, and you are very special.

Just because your mom is pregnant doesn't mean ▶ you can't do things together, just like always.

Do You Know About Babies?

What do you know about babies? You might think that babies only eat, sleep, and cry. But actually there's more to them than that. Babies will play with your fingers if you wiggle them where they can see them. They will move to look at you when you make a sound or when you softly touch them. You can even learn how you used to act from your new **sibling** (SIB-ling). Ask your mom or dad about when you were born. Ask to see pictures of yourself when you were a baby. Your parents will probably have funny stories to tell about when you were a baby.

◀ Spending time with your baby sister or brother can be fun for both of you.

9

Older or Younger?

You may wonder why your parents had another baby. Some parents have brothers or sisters, and want you to have that **experience** (ex-PEER-ee-ents) too. Some parents grew up alone, but don't want you to grow up alone. Ask your parents about their brothers and sisters. Their brothers and sisters are your uncles and aunts! Were your parents the oldest or the youngest kids in their families? If they were older, they could help you be a big brother or sister. If they were younger, you can find out what they liked about their older brothers and sisters.

Some siblings are very close to each other, just like their parents were. ▶

Being a Brother or Sister

You probably already know how to be a sister or brother, even if you've never been one. You know how to get along with new and different people. That's a big part of what siblings do. They try to get along and understand each other. That doesn't mean you'll always get along with your siblings. Ask anyone who has ever had a brother or sister! Sometimes you'll want to play with your new brother or sister. Sometimes you'll want to do something else. That's okay.

◀ With a brother or sister in your family, there's usually someone around to have fun with.

Babies Are Hard Work

After the baby is born, your mom will be very tired. And caring for the baby is hard too. Babies eat a lot. At first, your baby sister or brother might wake up each night to eat. Your mom or dad will get up to feed your baby brother or sister. Babies need help with other things too. They don't know how to sit, crawl, roll over, or talk. You can help your sibling with these things.

Your new brother or sister will learn very quickly that you are someone who will take care of him or her. ▶

What About Me?

It may seem like your parents are always helping the baby. They are always feeding, changing, and rocking the baby. Your family helped you when you were a baby too. You may not remember this time, because you were very little. But everything they do for the baby, they also did for you. They fed you and changed you and rocked you to sleep, just like the new baby. They helped you learn to walk and talk, just like the new baby. Remembering this can help you be **patient** (PAY-shunt) with your new brother or sister.

◀ New babies need a lot of attention from their mothers. When you were a baby, your mom spent a lot of time with you.

Your Feelings Are Important

People will spend a lot of time helping the baby. You might want some help too. People might say, "The baby doesn't know how to wait. But since you're older, we know you can."

You might not always want to wait. You might wish the baby would be quiet or even go away. You're not a bad person for feeling this way. Having a new member in the family can sometimes feel **uncomfortable** (un-KUMF-ter-buhl). If the baby upsets you, talk to your mom or dad about how you feel.

Talking to your mom or dad about your new brother or sister may make you feel better. ▶

Being a Teacher

Babies don't know how to talk when they are born. But you can think and talk about what you want or need. You can tell your mom or dad if you'd like a hug or help with your homework because they helped you learn how to talk. A baby will need help learning how to talk and understand, just like you did. You can be a teacher for your new brother or sister. Your new brother or sister will want to learn from you. And it will make you feel good that you taught him or her something important.

◀ Teaching new things to your new brother or sister can be fun for everyone in the family.

Good Changes

Having a new brother or sister means your family will be different than before. It may be very different or only a little different. No matter how much it changes, it can feel strange having a new person in the family. Talk to your mom or dad about your feelings and the changes in your family. Even though having a new sibling can mean many different things, your family is still the same. It's still a group of people who love and **support** (suh-PORT) each other, including you.

Glossary

experience (ex-PEER-ee-ents) Something that happens or occurs.

patient (PAY-shunt) Being able to put up with a difficult situation.

pregnant (PREG-nunt) When a female has an unborn baby growing inside her body.

sibling (SIB-ling) A brother or sister.

support (suh-PORT) To help.

uncomfortable (um-KUMF-ter-buhl) Feeling scared and unsure about something.

Index